THE EASTER WONDERS

Chloe E. Gore

Jesus arrived at the city of Jerusalem. As he rode in on a donkey, crowds of people greeted him with happy faces, 'Hooray!' The fame of Jesus spread throughout the country, and everyone knew that he was the King promised by God. So they shouted and cheered, waving palm branches. 'Hosanna! The man God has sent is here!'

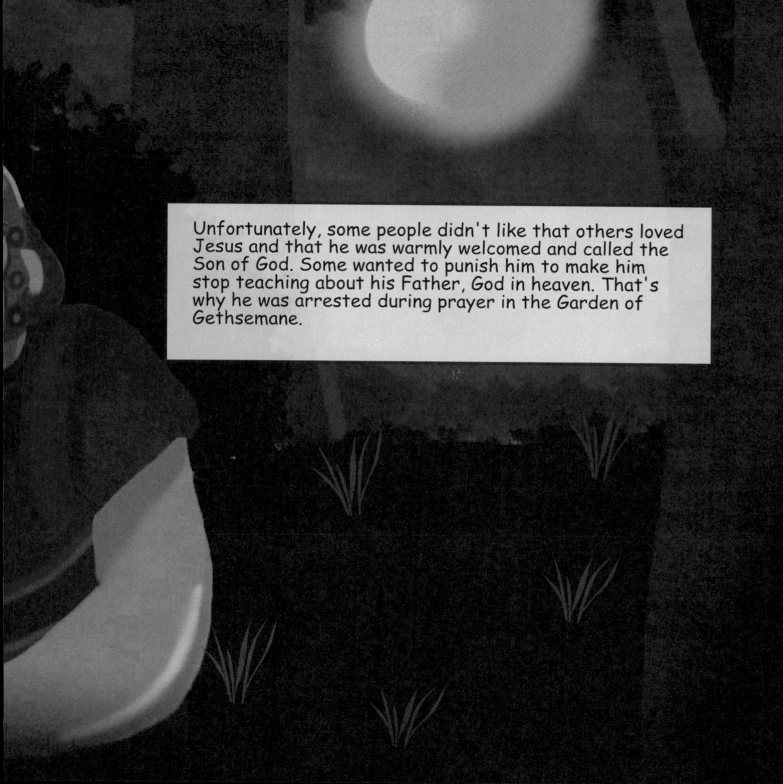

Unfortunately, some people didn't like that others loved Jesus and that he was warmly welcomed and called the Son of God. Some wanted to punish him to make him stop teaching about his Father, God in heaven. That's why he was arrested during prayer in the Garden of Gethsemane.

Jesus was brought before a great court where he was accused of things he did not do. Even though Pilate didn't want Jesus to die, he had to make a decision. He asked the crowd what he should do. Many people shouted, 'Crucify him!'

Jesus had difficulty carrying the heavy cross through the streets of Jerusalem. Many people mocked him, but there were also people who helped him. One of them was Veronica, who wiped his face, and the other was Simon of Cyrene, who assisted him in carrying the cross.

When Jesus reached the top of the mountain, called Golgotha, he was hung on the cross. Then the promise was fulfilled, and Jesus said, 'Father, **into Your hands I commit my spirit!**' This meant that he was giving his life for all people who live and will live. At that moment, the sky darkened.

The body of the Lord Jesus was placed in a tomb cut into the rock, and the entrance was sealed with a large stone.

Guards were stationed to prevent anyone from stealing the body.

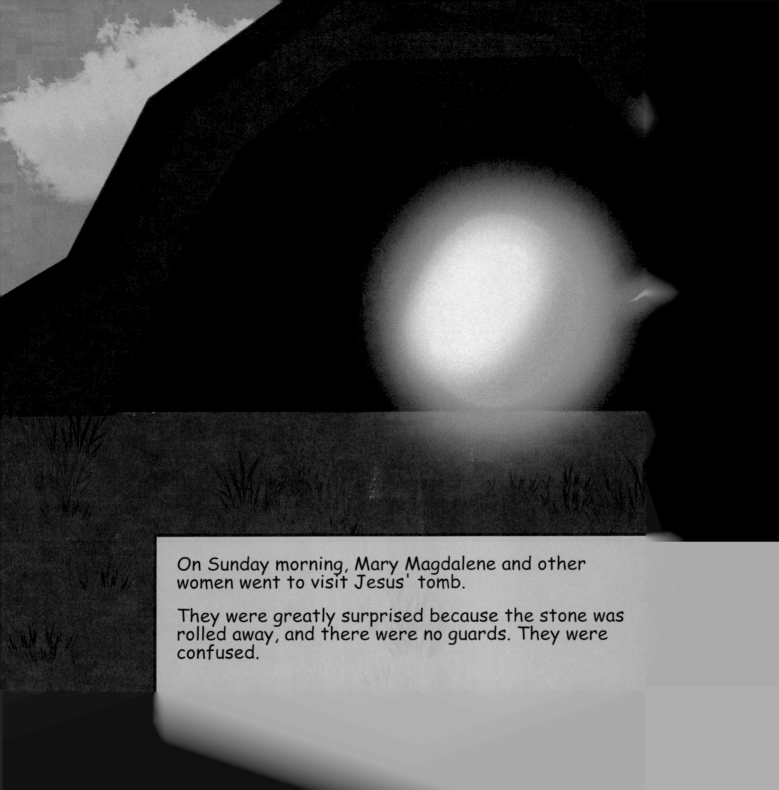

On Sunday morning, Mary Magdalene and other women went to visit Jesus' tomb.

They were greatly surprised because the stone was rolled away, and there were no guards. They were confused.

After a moment, an Angel appeared and addressed them: 'I know you are looking for Jesus, but he is not here. **Jesus is alive again, just as he promised!**'

The women were surprised by this message and couldn't believe their ears. They immediately ran to Jesus' friends to share this extraordinary news. '**Jesus is risen!**' they shouted. However, at first, people didn't believe them.

The disciples remembered that Jesus had previously told them about his death and promised that on the third day he would rise again. Although they didn't fully understand what he meant at the time, now, seeing that everything had been fulfilled according to his words, they believed in his power and promises.

Forty days later, Jesus unexpectedly appeared among his disciples. Some of them felt fear, but Jesus reassured them, saying, 'Don't be afraid! **I died, but now I am alive again!** Now go to all nations and tell this Good News.' The disciples were very happy. Then, Jesus bid them farewell, saying, **'I am going to my Father, but I will always be with you!'** At that moment, a cloud lifted him up to heaven.

The disciples set out on their journey, telling everyone they met about Jesus, the Son of God. Despite numerous difficulties, they continued to spread the message all over the world. In this way, the Gospel spread widely.

Today, we celebrate the death and resurrection of Jesus on Easter Sunday, thanking God for His promise of eternal life. It is a time of joy and hope as we remember the redeeming act of Christ and celebrate His victory over death, giving us hope for eternal salvation.